A Dire Shortage
of Usable Meaning

A Dire Shortage of Usable Meaning
Two Poems

Nathaniel Rudavsky-Brody

MadHat Press
Cheshire, Massachusetts

MadHat Press
MadHat Incorporated
PO Box 422, Cheshire, MA 01225

Copyright © 2024 Nathaniel Rudavsky-Brody
All rights reserved

The Library of Congress has assigned
this edition a Control Number of
2024930870

ISBN 978-1-952335-74-7 (paperback)

Words by Nathaniel Rudavsky-Brody
Cover image: Merovingian fibulae, Bossut-Gottechain. Musées royaux d'art et d'histoire, Brussels. Creative Commons CC by MRAH/KMKG.
Cover design by F. J. Bergmann

www.MadHat-Press.com

First Printing
Printed in the United States of America

For Sara

Table of Contents

Enclosure	1
Time (An Illusion of Place)	63
Acknowledgments	119
About the Author	121

Enclosure

Nathaniel Rudavsky-Brody

i

In the beginning there was
a garden, longer
than it was wide, and seeming
never to end since the place
where it joined the other gardens
stood for a forest,
with two chestnuts, a birch
and a tangle of
undergrowth consisting mainly
of ornamental shrubs
long gone to seed and their
unruly descendants.

A Dire Shortage of Usable Meaning

garden: *from guard, enclosure,*

Nathaniel Rudavsky-Brody

This garden was the good
in our lives, the only one
in a time when the leaf-curl of
creation was spent
in a quick
generation of thin-blooded
men, who all the days
of our lives drew blood
with their claims on
our lives, and our private
voices grew too faint
to matter; when the

A Dire Shortage of Usable Meaning

a space to be kept and kept clean and kept out of

Nathaniel Rudavsky-Brody

creation of a new
order, from the way, from
the simple fact
we touched,
began to resemble
the way
of the world, and we
the men and women
of the world, tired
of ourselves and of our
being tired
and most of all of the world

kept apart from the gardens of others
(good: a certain feeling when touched in a certain place;
waiting to be touched there) the state of whose finances

Nathaniel Rudavsky-Brody

as if a garden
was to be found,
not lost. I saw
you learn what living
years in the wiser,
truer world
had never taught you;
you saw the
stutter of
seasons repeat itself
a year later,
yourself unmoved

A Dire Shortage of Usable Meaning

is seen, like the stained soul parodied
in a stained shirt, by the state of their lawn, their half of the hedge,
(the good: a certain idea you had
as a girl of what it meant to mean something,

(unchanged, I mean,
unchanged)
and you grew wise to
the words that do not mean
as much as a morning
reading, your knees drawn up
in an old wicker chair
salvaged from somewhere,
in the chill of the sun,
even the late rose
insignificant
(unsignifying, I mean)

*a triangulation of Dostoevsky
and the frog prince) the tragic yaw
between what they plant with all good intentions
and what they manage to keep (creation:
what hides inside us, decides us, after what strained to meaning
is spent, and we fall back naked
and failed on the barely recognizable sheets) in state*

A Dire Shortage of Usable Meaning

the sun: *waiting*
rose: *a flower*

Nathaniel Rudavsky-Brody

ii

Outside,
the roads ran fast
with the errands of
people who did not
cease to exist
simply because we, young
or unwise, had come
to a tacit
understanding with
the ways of the world,
feigning a time
when they did not exist yet.

A Dire Shortage of Usable Meaning

tacit: *but where to begin,
so much is unspoken*

Nathaniel Rudavsky-Brody

We knew that the road
was waiting, for a glance
or an unwise press
of the fingers on skin,
on paper, or for when the grass,
so green with the sop
and slant light of
autumn that it threw back
reflections of the broad leaves
waiting to fall,
would have drunk too much blood
from our hands.

*putting it down on paper, putting it to
music (dead leaves: but did I tell you about
the moment when the hills are turned to red water?)*

Nathaniel Rudavsky-Brody

When the grass
of your rented garden
is as saturated
as a low-lying field
in the autumn of this
cold place
you will be turned out,
you will take your place
again in the rooms of cards,
a cafe will be your
rest, a park
where lindens and plane trees

A Dire Shortage of Usable Meaning

is no way to redress (reflection:
your answer was not, as I expected, the leaves falling
one by one on the grass that was as blank as a mirror)
the dire shortage of usable meaning

Nathaniel Rudavsky-Brody

embower the gutted
drunks as the well-bred hurry
past with their dogs
will be your share
of the world's abundance:
you were never one of them
to share in the shifty
labors of their
soggy fields or the fruit
of their orchards passed
in fragments from father to shiftless
son,

or (blood: an unequal measure)
is the perfect silence
of the leaves on this gray, windless morning
the same silence of bodies,

Nathaniel Rudavsky-Brody

though you may know the son—
so we heard, in
the reassurance,
the guttural drag
of our neighbors' cars,
priceless though they were,
more intimate for knowing there was
no chance they would let us stay
after they had taken their share,
knowing they would spurn us
with gentle words, reassuring
unambiguous words

*their contractual movements wise to leaving a word
unsaid as the only way to avoid
coming face to face with misunderstanding*

your bodies were young then
(priceless: but how to recall
the calculations we made, the prices we set)

Nathaniel Rudavsky-Brody

iii

But this city was
waiting for us
since the beginning,
waiting for us to
emerge from our
private idea of the good,
waiting to accept
our submission
to its interminable
logic with hardly
a knowing glance.
I had seen leaves fall,

waiting: *itself a knowledge, or intimation*
or figuration or
vague premonition of the good

Nathaniel Rudavsky-Brody

and seeds fall
where saplings will crowd
the vanishing point
of a narrow
garden, but turning
again to the city, I
saw the falling seed
of an ash tree scud
against a brick wall,
an interrupted curve,
and land on the sidewalk,
less light than consequence,

A Dire Shortage of Usable Meaning

*no, a remembered profile of the good,
a woman glimpsed on the tram who you thought
would make me happy, though you knew,
discounting time, I would never meet her because
I do not take the same tram as you
did, going to work on those our first mornings*

Nathaniel Rudavsky-Brody

I saw
men swing from their
death-heavy truck
to collect the green plastic
bags of leaves
set out as an offering
before the houses,
empty rituals
asking to be swept
clean of their guilt
and released from their
neighbors' good

*no, a profile, perhaps, but forgetting
how the abstract becomes body when it
is close enough to touch and we let
ourselves (and how
a body becomes idea again after the
night that only engenders new waiting)*

Nathaniel Rudavsky-Brody

graces, I even saw trees
growing were there is
no soil, only unpainted
echoing chambers
of guilt, signed mazes
to hide the unnatural
vehicles of their
lusts: those signs
of trees so thinly
imagined by the
pale architects of that place
they did not embarrass

elision of form with fact, the friction of fact, the fact of
a body
entering
another

Nathaniel Rudavsky-Brody

the concrete, clean as slate,
with leaves;
though just to be safe
they closed their
office windows
as one, to reflect
the sky, so the fall,
the falling off,
the failing
of leaves
could safely be
overlooked

*no, the sea-change of justice after the fact
or when the facts change
(others let go, but you, but I,
do not believe in time)*

A Dire Shortage of Usable Meaning

no

Nathaniel Rudavsky-Brody

iv
Or is this the world
I was waiting for,
the sea-glass globe
turning way
at the end of the long, straight-edged
street, the light falling
forward and down around
the razor edge of
the city with all the
accumulated weight
of its gear-works, of
work;

A Dire Shortage of Usable Meaning

razor: *a word whose meaning, since it was
sheathed in protective plastic, is inaccessible,
rendering such expressions
moot, or at best unusable or at worst
harmless, I say worst since what is more dire
than words whose misuse cannot slice open the onion-
skins of the body*

Nathaniel Rudavsky-Brody

we were waiting for,
all the live-long dimly
lit day indoors
so that walking
still far from home
the black-lit avenue,
black cars gliding
around the blind bend like dreams,
the occasional face an
unexpected hitch
in the dream turning away as I
pass, turning to glance

*as the male sexual organ, sheathed in protective plastic,
is less definitive (razor: how our fathers started their
every day in the chill of mythic mornings,
in the aureate glare of bathroom light,
years when the blade was already sheathed in plastic
but flimsier plastic and with the projected touch of my small fingers
I imagined the blade as the grain of truth
in the story at hand*

Nathaniel Rudavsky-Brody

at panes of light that are only
the ground-level doorways to higher
planes of domestic
bliss (still empty
at this hour,
and the cars are always black,
these people have money)
I am spending
our final grace;
is this the knowledge
of ourselves we were
hoping to break

*as later I went looking for grains of truth
in all the usual places (razor:
no longer of philosophical use*

Nathaniel Rudavsky-Brody

through to
when we supposed the fruit
must be the fruit of
something, and did not believe
that a fall from
grace could simply
exist, like a dent
in the sidewalk
or a climate
or a part of speech,
but had to be earned,
we reasoned,

*now philosophy is worn away by use
and no longer serves to protect
from use the eloquence of the body
(or some would say
the end of philosophy
and birth-cut of a world of
efficient cause*

Nathaniel Rudavsky-Brody

when we believed
that a slow death in exile
was something that happened
far from home?
God, send rain,
a little cold rain
that we may die
in the rain
as it was intended,
but nothing is final
anymore, not even
this rain

*since once the efficient cause has
been singled out, it can be cut
off, as by wearing a condom
instead of threading the contradictions,
the obligations, the stories of each night out (razor:*

Nathaniel Rudavsky-Brody

v

The hardest part
of the story was not
being sent away from
the garden into
a world of scrub pines
and hard work,
but when their children
found that the world was
set in its ways,
the main points of
geography already
settled

children: *who were the renunciation of their knowledge,*

Nathaniel Rudavsky-Brody

and the mill-house,
caved and cluttered
and its wheel wrenched
off, still
inhabited,
as if by a fusty,
handy giant
from an earlier
generation

who found them out (cluttered: *with spare parts*)

Nathaniel Rudavsky-Brody

and your first house
still bright on the hill,
and your second
house damp
in the shadow of
a block of new flats,
locked,
small as a
broken toy

A Dire Shortage of Usable Meaning

(locked: *empty*)

Nathaniel Rudavsky-Brody

and all the roads
to the airport
traveled at some
time or
another, yet
you are still
here

A Dire Shortage of Usable Meaning

if only time

Nathaniel Rudavsky-Brody

when we have
flown,
what will
remain
of our
visions?

A Dire Shortage of Usable Meaning

were an equal

measure

Time (An Illusion of Place)

The Blind Leave behind the Blind

Though I lived there, I did not feel
what efforts the earth had made to repress
its old opinions.

Grade and contour squeezed
to a residue of night-sweat, trying
to seem level-headed and sure.

I did not see that the people
were the long waking dream
of the earth, their faces honed
by no contrast of a better life.

The sky, without the competition
of shined windows and steel,
was bluer than I could ever get used to.

Nathaniel Rudavsky-Brody

*

Riding the tram out,
they delayed as long as possible,
straight and still in their seats,
changing their faces.

All this you know. But do
you know those buildings and streets and painted storefronts
refusing the eye like a white mid-winter haze?

*

The tram we rode there,
the oldest in the whole city,
had forgotten even to be sorry.

It riddled its tracks like memories
of old back pains and gout
down vertebrae packed in the dirt.

Like memories of injury and unclear memories.

Like all the unsure ailments packed in the dirt
that will not, like winter's scaly bulbs,
brave the air again.

*

I left behind me something unheard-of,
old people happy
in the cheap burnish of windows.

Coffee at eight and beer at eleven
warmed their faces like plate glass
as the windows clouded like troubled faces.

At the end of that square, pale-lit or rain-lit,
the door of the church was a grating
that caught and held and saved up the wind's litter.

At eight and eleven and four it was always closed.

Seventh-Century Christ

They didn't get it right.
The straightness of his lines
is itself
a kind of nudity
and he is naked
but there is no pain in his eyes,
his muscles don't turn
from the pain they deflower
in those who open to him
their miserable lives.
No one was saved
by his blank strength.
No one is saved.

Tell things as they are.

Say it is a map of graves dug up (to be emptied in rows of ill-fitting wooden drawers)

in a place called Saint Anne's Field, which in 1891 is being erased, name and all,

by two or three washes of brick townhouses and a few small manufactures.

Still, I will repeat that it is the earth tallying, crooked and haphazard,

in a schoolboy's handwriting, the numbers of the dead it never asked to be asked to file away.

Numbers and not number, since the earth has a goldfinch's memory and keeps starting over,

a new row of studious ticks a little higher up, or off to the left,

fully intending to get it right this time, and each time losing count and having to begin again,

but never entirely from scratch, no, never from scratch.

Begin again. There are 261 squared-off lozenges diving like angry starlings

from the upper right-hand corner, though the occasional smaller lozenge turns up against the slanted flight of its fellows, or else is tucked in a corner, with no regard

for orientation; and this hurried downward flight beats past and around

and through three or four sets of thick lines that enclose no space,

finish in no corners or cornerstones or conclusions,

all bounded by a blank strip which looks rather like a canal but is labeled the highway to M.

What are they diving at so full of anger?

No attempt is made to suggest an outside or a beyond.

Whatever the surroundings, to spite topography scratch out that label and write highway

to heaven, or road to hell, or love canal.

Schoolboy's lingo but truth as well, where later you would have gone, but didn't.

Hardscrabble paper. Inexistent numbers. Say it is a rough draft for forgetting,

and still I'll repeat that it's a ledger of wished-for and expired futures.

Nathaniel Rudavsky-Brody

Change of Currency

Since we were small,
we tried
a modest idea of travel.

Our destination was no further
than where the city forgets itself
and goes to seed.

Where countryside waits for concrete
and asphalt to pass as a cat
waits for a shadow to pass.

Where patience is fatal and the bird
an illusion.

*

The train carried away
the sense of purpose
we were counting on to make it through.

At the station we found no signs
of where the center was,
or whether we were seeking the center.

If the road had any opinions
it kept them to itself
and stared blankly down the road.

*

Finding no friend among those buildings
we took comfort
in putting our trust in others
and their bad decisions.

We only trusted ourselves to recognize
where today's mindless lines would converge
in what yesterday had failed to say.

Only the distant ranks
of traffic-lights, changing their colors
in stymied time, kept faith.

*

Away from the main road,
noise was compromised
by the inanities of silence.

A playing-field,
all liquid resentment now it was empty,
lapped at dry sidewalks.

It reflected the dusk
as green as glass as green
as a pond somewhere.

Nathaniel Rudavsky-Brody

*

We'd come looking for a past
held in the palm of a small present,
but found the palm wide open
and greased with a rough idea of speed.

Only that intrepid trio,
the bank, the bar, and the grill-house,
were real.

The old tower was stuffed
with blackened scaffolding like an owl
stuffed with sawdust and impious thoughts.

If the ground under it
once held something more human,
we could not tell.

*

I can remember no color
except the fluorescent leer
of a twice-misleading landmark.

And the greens of the evening's
reflection in the grass.

And the shades of those stones rejected by evening.

Nathaniel Rudavsky-Brody

What was found there. They want details.

A cramped rectangular space under the demolished church, for instance.

With ten aligned tombs, for instance. Three of which held women's hip-bones,

for instance, but only one a magnificent gold brooch and amber beads,

and only one a damascene silver brooch, and only one a coin that recalls Charon's obol

but was found not on the tongue, but near her hand,

as if when she arrived at the dark river she would make the fatal transaction herself,

and not wait for the ferryman's fingers, calloused and bloated

from an eternity of rowing both ways across the forgetfulness of the damned,

to pry the toll from her delicate, cold mouth.

Twenty-four pins and clasps and brooches of silver and bronze and bone,

and none of them clasping or pinning so much as a modest second thought.

Two sword-blades, one throwing-ax, fourteen knives of various forms and sizes and how many spear-points again? A glass jar whose four uneven handles like octopus arms

had the impossible delicacy of the truly second-rate, imported from a country

which he whose broken feet it was found at

would have imagined with a forward-leaning nostalgia

for its vineyards and women who belonged neither to his past nor his future,

but very well could have, but for a subtle change in the vast currents of populations

or an unexpected gust of individual motion. For instance.

What wasn't found there, is a much easier question to answer.

Nathaniel Rudavsky-Brody

After the Flood

Think of the dove
who flies three times into
an emptiness, and the third time
stays there, alone.

Think of the man who stands
with his hands empty, watching the sky.

And of us, behind him,
unable to follow his gaze,
who, seeing a sign in that vague expansion,
believe the rain is over.

They Found Us Sleeping

i.

What will they do, when they
have measured these swords,

these blades tempered in clay
and rainwater, these spearheads forged

in spring run-off
and sword-belts dissolved

to the very color of clay at the
touch of clay? When they take

in their calipers' keen grasp,
and the open palm of their scales,

the many measures
of coastlines, briared and wooded,

where edges of dagger and ax
have lost their gift of persuasion

to the years which came
like downdraft and rising breeze

of a single short evening?
As if the erosion,

Nathaniel Rudavsky-Brody

the rock-shelf and landslide of rivers
were waiting for them,

only them, in the metal's stripped
and flaking and matted leaves, and even

the arc and angle of our borrowed sky,
though the lashes of hide

that held it
fast to the same polestar,

alone and faint in its quiet patch
of darkness bearing the blows of friends,

have long, like the sword-belts and our own
sinews, gone slack,

leaving no trace but the mute impression of
necessity.

For in these woods, each man
was a friend, if that name

may mean one whose deep,
deep eyes you believed at first sight

without understanding
or needing to understand.

A Dire Shortage of Usable Meaning

Those dearer friends for whom
we paused on the shallow incline

of evening, and waited until they came close,
their eyes sunk in the lost light of their faces,

were those in the end
who hurt us. Their lesson could not be refused

but there was no time to learn it,
indeed, there was no time

between their last touch, fatal and light,
and the blankness into which they disappeared.

What will they do, when they
have weighed even the colors

of the beads that lay
as if fallen and rolled to rest

under our fallen ribs,
and tuned the silk cord

that carried them,
gone like a spider's crossing—

what, is it so soon morning?
The field where we lost our whorled

Nathaniel Rudavsky-Brody

and worthless beads is held fast
by houses squatting in concrete,

but here in the garden
there are new filaments tying the hedge

to the chair, which over the long night rusted
and sank deeper into the grass,

dewed with no less
marvelous beads: a sign

that as we wake, overtaken
by new disorder,

the things of this world that claim
our divided care are too numerous.

Let us refuse them, blind as we are
and hearing only the wind

playing its ragtimes harshly
through branches black-brushed

on the shadows of these brick walls,
the wind that whips the grassed

half-contours of our lonely shale selves.
And let us listen, listen

for the twang of taut silk
and other impossible musics.

ii.

Without love, you had said,
the body isn't beautiful.

You were, by then, under six feet
of dirt and the rubble of other false starts.

Still, your voice across the mixed-up
strata of time was clear;

then why did we listen, not to you
but to our minds that, sure of their step,

slipped in with the heavy and quick push
of desire; why did we reach

to touch what could not mean
what it was supposed to mean; why

did we hold so little back
when we were touched?

As if that were the way of things,
the way

to float our separate and future lives
over the land, braced

against fear and the unpredictable updrafts of air,
and create, in that airborne moment of choice

between different angles of sun and truth,
our selves. As if we simply refused to choose.

But the moment passed,
the vantage was lost

and we, our own survivors, were left
with the nothing we surely always meant:

no pocketed souvenir,
no creased map from the empty welcome booth,

no tickets for the next guided visit,
no rain-check, no guide

to putting the bits of bones of you that remain
back together. And that's

why every time made us die
another disheveled lifetime, another day:

you have to figure it out yourself,
and one of the screws goes missing,

you find they gave you the wrong glue, or a key
piece falls to dust, and none of the rest makes sense,

Nathaniel Rudavsky-Brody

though they were you once, these bones.
Here where we stand,

here where we lie to ourselves,
is no middle ground,

not even a resting place, since the dumber,
kinder love (a sister's kiss, long dead,

a mother's survival) which stowed us in stone
or wood or cloth achievements, thinking it did us good,

that love, exposed to the elements,
lasted less long than our harder elements.

It stands to reason either
that there is no love here, since these bodies

are not beautiful, or that
even the smallest fragment

invokes the whole, sublime in its
force and shear and lost economy,

our every night alone with other eyes,
met or unmet, taken or lost

or dreamed, even the ones that made us
a lie to ourselves, even our every

morning of lies. Who,
I ask you, who can resist such reason

now the body is old, and only the mind
is left to seek, by its own devices, rest?

Now that the mind grows weak, and rages
against its dying that all was fair,

that it was all beautiful? That's life,
we say, now we are washed away by rain

we cannot chance or choose. But no,
I will not make peace with our

other lives. Until I can hide you,
guiltless against our guilt,

I will resist this soil that holds
me every day closer to its own elements.

No, I will linger here in this soil,
and proclaim, simply by being here,

to be found or not (as if that mattered)
that without this body no love is ever beautiful,

one bone of me, one bone
of you somewhere, blind and impossibly far

Nathaniel Rudavsky-Brody

keeping faith. For you it matters. Better to yield
yourself to the absent mind of the soil

than to hands breaking the soil,
the eyes and measures of men,

their guilt so deep
that they are blind to our own.

iii.

When you turned in your sleep,
two garnets, gold-set

with bits of glass and local stones,
stayed where they were, separated

from you by dark, impossible inches.
True, you were always losing earrings,

it seemed you had a whole box of those
whose seconds had slipped off or been

forgotten when you slipped off,
but they were only the breadcrumbs and stones

you left to mark the way back,
not to the beginning of life but to

some moment, lost, of its branching.
This was, I think,

a deliberate loss, your act
of renunciation (late but not too late)

by which you always said
you'd join me. Not that I mean to

Nathaniel Rudavsky-Brody

make light of what you had already
released into the vague erasure

of all that we ignore when we're dead,
though right beside us. Not that I think

myself so light. But watching
you fall away from this last piece

touching your breastbone where once
it touched your breast, I saw

how mere metallic touch
can mean, and dispel, a world.

Even the dead, I know, have needs,
one of which is beauty, though a beauty tuned

to close quarters and lack of air
and the constant, irritating tickle of sand,

and there is no notion of distance here,
so I can only conceive of details

which never change or multiply
or come to succeed us, summing to more than ourselves,

and my eyes have adjusted to no darkness,
since at every sift or shift

absurdly I hoped to see you
and my vanished pupils stayed small

to direct that light.
Not once, waiting against

the dark that ever renewed itself
with new false promise, did I remember

to cry out to my lord,
as we had rehearsed in the interminable play,

even to cry out questions like who it was
that slept in the dark so near at hand,

who turned in her sleep, pursued
by dreams of erasure and one persistent

desire, to renounce, to renounce
before the night grew tired and lost

its way to dawn. As it did in the end.
As all our nights did, in the end.

Those garnets were eyes
of a fierce and inscrutable bird

whose wings were knotted like metro lines,
its claws grasping, as grammar's rules

Nathaniel Rudavsky-Brody

press words in line despite both their sense and ours,
the folded cloth that kept you together

for other eyes. It is
no madness, now we have been

deconstellated to bracken and bones,
to believe an ornament conceals

our nakedness, your breasts, fallen,
my insufficient flesh.

And when it is lost,
pure madness to try to remember

the relief of walking dressed
and holding your head high

now that the shame of dreams has won.
I cannot remember

the artist's eye, that saw
in the uncut and cloudy stones

the soul of a bird, and made it
see for a while, with what erring art he had,

nor the named
and nameless men who on roads

of the sea brought careful handfuls of stones
from a south which, held

in the earth's cold oven, we can no longer invent.
That is all. The real

of red suspended in its own light
escapes us, as it always did in the end,

and who would dare dream further,
who would dare understand?

Nathaniel Rudavsky-Brody

iv.

Lying now in the morning, you turn
but do not open your eyes.

You are as I remember,
though your face is harder,

concentrated on cracking
some illogical nut

of a dream grown small and dry
behind your eyelids.

You are wearing no final
resolution of mind or will

which you relinquished once as the toll
to sleep; you are wearing nothing

but warm skin that turns
away, tending

not to my warmth which waits,
but to a coolness

which only you can discern
in the linen light which only you can discern

in the room which does not exist,
not yet. For whom

are you undressed? Or rather,
for whom as the earth unmade you:

whose gaze, though blind,
must read the slope and splay,

the folds and negligence
of your body before

you let yourself be held,
and, held in my arms, assume

what's left of the self when that understanding
has been lifted and taken away?

And what will they do, now
they have taken the brooch

that fell away, the earrings fallen away,
cold and thin among folds of sheets,

folds of earth, clods and runnels of sheets,
tokens and thimbles,

and your belt broken down
to golden disks strung like irregular stars?

Nathaniel Rudavsky-Brody

As if there was something waiting for them,
only them, to read

in the metal flaking apart like leaves,
or as if we were waiting

for them to take us up by the hand, kind angels,
and in exchange for our sleep

absolve us of waiting.
After the squall,

a long and steady and quiet rain
bends left and right the flowering chestnut,

still raising its thick candles.
Though this be an elegy for roads taken,

and for an idea of a city, if not for a city,
we cannot hurry the rain, which will fall

until its dwindling. The roots
that drink this rain

will keep, I think, their word.
They will hold and will not pry, break down

yet not undress
the lives that are stowed unchanging there,

other lives, perhaps, but that seek
like us in the absent mind of the soil

only the absolution
of not being found

by hands breaking the soil,
the eyes and measures of men,

their guilt so deep, my dear,
that they are blind to our own.

Nathaniel Rudavsky-Brody

Last Judgment

Clear skies make
it easier to
accept
this long
light.
The day

dying more slowly
than we do gives
us a feather
to preen, a
reason
to strut.

Tonight
though, clouds,
like autumn's,
slide miles
into
the penumbra

of our just
deserts.
We know
what we have done.

Except they were never waiting to be found. Otherwise we would be gods,

and our rows of ill-fitting wooden drawers, the hecatomb of truth,

and museums a promise,

free from population pressures and past engagements and the dried blood of words.

Otherwise truth would indeed be beautiful, if not beauty itself as some would have it,

and you could hear the bones rising into the heavens of our intellectual gaze.

I have spent my life like a cornered politician or a jealous lover,

waiting for amnesty from truth through a semblance of pain,

or from pain through a semblance of truth. The earth, emptied of dead

and freed of their odd angles and last unsatisfied whims, would be earth again.

Yet my only foray into politics was to speak aloud, and feel my words being heard,

my school of jealousy was the unlearned lesson that a woman was not myself,

that her life did not coincide with mine, nor her mind.

Nathaniel Rudavsky-Brody

Otherwise our learning could absolve them, and our insight console them,

and our scholarly papers be letters of safe conduct for their souls.

Eurydice

Her face was veiled, with what
was too simple for words.

I saw there, moving like shades
in a kingdom of shades,

the sheaf of faces, or faceless
indeterminate time

and when she followed me back
to the light of what

had been ours, I turned
and saw she was

not following: no,
her steps were for herself,

slow and unerring and light as leaves.
She knew the way.

Nathaniel Rudavsky-Brody

A Wall, as in a Mirror

We wanted to go further
but the city kept us, a tangle of string
it couldn't shake from its hands.

Nights, we tried our hardest to dream
of frosted valleys and time
issuing from the mouths of cattle.

Days, we tried to remember
whether or not we had dreamed.

Satisfied with our own evasive answers.

*

We spent whole days making plans
to visit valleys we identified
in the clutter of maps.

We went through atlases
like loves in an endless lost spring
or plans in a deluded middle age.

We were betrayed by their pages
into nearly believing the truth,
or regretting a view of the world
so casually tossed off.

Thankfully we found others
so densely printed
their truths were unreadable.

Nathaniel Rudavsky-Brody

*

The smallest space of color
between the names
and the lines filled me
with terror of perpetual motion.

I turned to you for help
but saw in your eyes the
same evasive answer.

Tonight, said those eyes,
our dreams will bring
new names but no new things.

*

We stared so long at train tables
the numbers became words and words
a parody of the world of the senses.

Rearranged, they might have made
one good sentence
in the evasive light of stations.

One landscape viewed from the platform
with birds pulled
downward by their disinterest
through habitual air.

We stared so long they became
stone walls worn down by time
and the breath of cattle.

Nathaniel Rudavsky-Brody

*

How can a map be real,
you always wanted to ask.

You were not questioning
the correspondence of signs
to the world of the senses.

We cannot read, between
the lines of states and imagined rivers,
the paper's reasons.

Musée de Cluny

She's gone to work. I stand
in her room that is closed
like the boxes I saw,
small chests and coffers
with their elaborate locks, and
reliquaries emptied
of magic: so many, it seemed
the whole museum
was given over to those small
failures to keep close
what never belonged. She's gone
to work. The cat,
forgetting for once what it means
to be closed in, watches
through the cracked-open
window, soft
miscellanies of rain.

She asks (herself anonymous now) how so-and-so is getting along,

she speaks a name, a piece of fruit picked up and held for a moment of indecision

and then put back, that might have ripened or rotted or stayed green

from the unseasonably cool weather or all the products they put on fruit nowadays. (Pausing

on the beveled edge of the afternoon that forces its way in through the kitchen window

while wonder bodies then vanishes like a glint of sun deep in the uneven glass.)

I came across pieces in a museum once whose provenance I recognized.

I had been by that river of abandoned steel mills. I had walked past that hill which,

from the banks, blocked the view of an unkempt highlands.

I had wondered what the obscurer of others had to hide.

Thick trees, a logging road far too wide for an isolated promontory.

A clearing where the ground was broken with the foundations of houses melting back into mud

despite the flapping gray tarps that looked two or three
 seasons old.

Still, I remained innocent. The downward slope, the alluvial
 plain reaching inland

between further hills, a farm re-painted to maintain its
 centuries-old propriety,

and then a drainage run edged by rotten and cloven ash trees:

so much uncontainable novelty, I forgot what I'd almost
 touched,

now cast over my right shoulder like salt or learning.

Nathaniel Rudavsky-Brody

Remembering What the Sea Is Like

They say the waves there fall
as many times as they climb and still
something is left in the cupped
hands of the rocks, some
light of unraveling threads
over a teaspoon of sand, a few
incurious fish, the repeating
fingers of a sea-
anemone there
where begin and end
and begin again reflections
of the small and imperfect
and more than perfect world.

Where Only Death Is a Metaphor

At last, on a final
evasive Sunday,
we travel for real.

There are distances, we find,
that cannot be conceived
in terms of distance.

There are places whose whole strangeness
is the heat of the sun
on chilled skin.

The particular shade of plane trees
whose every leaf is a silence
and a cry of children at play.

Nathaniel Rudavsky-Brody

*

Here the morning unfolds
its paper and passes
the morning reading.

The sea is in no hurry
to warm to the sky's
ambitious plans.

It has all day to fulfill
its role as mirror to one
decisive idea.

*

The evening has no use
for a dimming sun.

It has eyes only
for its own advent, and lets
the sun run out in a country of hills.

They were there all along,
but following the brighter argument
we did not see them.

Soon we too will go into hills
but soon is an idea
whose meaning we have forgotten.

*

Climbing away from the coast,
the changed season believes
it has saved us.

We have been mistaken
for seedlings whose only needs
are heat and moisture.

If only the right breeze
can be found, we will be transformed.

*

We have no need for the past.

Maybe we are slipping
into happiness,
or maybe the end.

Without old stones as our measure,
how can we tell if this
is merely a visit, or a new life?

If we have really given the slip
to our lives,

or if this is only
the long waking dream
of the earth?

Acknowledgments

Excerpts from "Time (An Illusion of Place)" were published in *Literary Imagination,* under the title "Against Archaeology."

About the Author

NATHANIEL RUDAVSKY-BRODY was born in Columbus, Ohio. His translations of French literature have been praised by reviewers in magazines and journals such as the *London Review of Books*, *The New York Review of Books*, *The Los Angeles Review*, *French Studies* and *Translation Review*. Recent publications include *The Idea of Perfection: The Poetry and Prose of Paul Valery* (FSG, 2020) and Benjamin Fondane's *Ulysses* (Syracuse, 2017), which received the Susan Sontag Prize for Translation. His translation of Lucien Rebatet's novel *The Two Standards* will be published by FSG in 2025. He is the author of two books of poetry in French, *Même la langue* and *En lieu de silence*, and has worked as a typesetter, a programmer, a teacher, and a private tutor in Greece.

Printed in the USA
CPSIA information can be obtained
at www.ICGtesting.com
LVHW050537121124
796295LV00002B/358